FIJI 2016 HUMAN RIGHTS REPORT

EXECUTIVE SUMMARY

Fiji is a constitutional republic. The country held general elections, which the Australian-led Multi-national Observer Group deemed credible and "broadly reflected the will of the Fijian people," in 2014. Josaia Voreqe (Frank) Bainimarama's Fiji First party won 32 of the 50 seats, and he was sworn in as prime minister.

Civilian authorities maintained effective control over the security forces.

The leading human rights problems included violence and discrimination against women, abuse of persons in custody, and subpar prison conditions.

Other human rights problems included restrictions on freedoms of speech and assembly, government corruption, sexual exploitation of children, and deep ethnic divisions, limited building access for persons with disabilities, and reports of forced labor. Workers in some industries, notably the security, transportation, and shipping sectors, worked excessive hours, and many work areas did not meet safety standards.

The government increasingly took steps to investigate security forces officials who committed abuses, and prosecuted or punished most officials who committed abuses elsewhere in the government. Impunity was a problem.

Section 1. Respect for the Integrity of the Person, Including Freedom from:

a. Arbitrary Deprivation of Life and other Unlawful or Politically Motivated Killings

There were no reports that the government or its agents committed arbitrary or unlawful killings.

On November 11, Justice Aruna Aluthge convicted the nine security force members (eight police officers and a military officer) involved in the 2014 rape, sexual assault, and death of robbery suspect Vilikesa Soko on all charges. On November 22, the judge sentenced each of them to prison ranging from seven to nine years.

b. Disappearance

There were no reports of politically motivated disappearances.

c. Torture and Other Cruel, Inhuman, or Degrading Treatment or Punishment

The constitution and the crimes decree prohibit torture, forced medical treatment, and degrading treatment or punishment. The Public Order Act Amendment Decree (POAD), however, authorizes the government to use whatever force it deems necessary to enforce public order. There were reports of security force members abusing individuals during the year.

On June 13, a joint police and armed military drug farm raid in the rural Viti Levu highlands led to the apprehension of 10 men, four of whom pled guilty to charges of unlawful cultivation of illicit drugs. One of the men, Alipate Saudranu, alleged police officers beat him while detained. Saudranu submitted a formal complaint with the Fiji Human Rights and Antidiscrimination Commission (FHRADC) against police.

Subsequently, on July 12, photos circulated on social media alleging that security forces tortured suspects during another drug farm raid. In response, Police Commissioner Sitiveni Qiliho said, and victims confirmed, the raid occurred in 2009. Police investigation into this 2009 case continued at year's end.

Investigations into the alleged abuse of Sakiusa Niulala by a 20-person police team in March 2015 remained pending at year's end.

Prison and Detention Center Conditions

Prison conditions did not meet international standards. The national prison system was overcrowded, with deteriorating infrastructure and complaints about delivery of essential services.

Physical Conditions: As in previous years, prisons were somewhat overcrowded, holding 1,423 inmates in facilities intended for 1,000. Authorities generally separated pretrial detainees and convicted prisoners at shared facilities, although in some cases authorities held them together. Prison facilities were not suited to inmates with physical and mental disabilities.

In December the Fiji Corrections Service terminated a corrections officer who allegedly raped a female inmate at the Labasa corrections facility. Police were still investigating the case at year's end.

The system had insufficient beds, inadequate sanitation, and a shortage of other basic necessities. Government officials reported two inmate deaths during the year: the first was attributable to inmate suicide, and the second was 65-year-old Kalivati Bakani, who died while being hospitalized for a terminal medical illness.

Administration: The Fiji Corrections Service (FCS) arranged outside job placements for inmates with less than one year of their sentence remaining to ease their return to society. FCS also used compulsory supervision orders, under which authorities could release inmates with less than a year to serve into the community to serve at a local church or other community center.

The constitution authorizes an Office of Accountability and Transparency (formerly known as the Ombudsman's Office) to investigate maladministration in government departments. Authorities had not legally established the office by year's end.

Prisoners may submit complaints to the FHRADC, which investigated a few such complaints during the year. Prisoners may also lodge complaints with the FCS and with visiting judges and magistrates when they inspect prisons.

The law allows prisoners to submit complaints to judicial authorities, but the government reviews all prisoner letters and, in most cases, has the authority to seize them. The law prohibits authorities from reviewing, censoring, or seizing prisoner letters to the FHRADC, but authorities routinely reviewed such letters. Authorities did not investigate or document credible allegations of inhuman conditions in a publicly accessible manner.

Independent Monitoring: During the year the International Committee of the Red Cross, the Office of the UN High Commissioner for Human Rights, and the FHRADC visited official detention facilities and interviewed inmates; prison authorities permitted such visits without third parties present.

Improvements: In February the FCS began construction on a new 200-inmate-capacity remand center to alleviate overcrowding at the corrections facility in Lautoka.

According to government officials, prison authorities recruited two psychologists, some senior medical officers, doctors, and nurses for employment full time at prison facilities to improve inmates' access to medical services.

d. Arbitrary Arrest or Detention

The constitution provides for protection against arbitrary arrest or detention. The Criminal Procedure Decree details procedures for lawful arrest. The POAD authorizes security forces to detain a person for up to 16 days before bringing charges; the minister of defense must authorize detention without charge exceeding 48 hours. There were no reports of unlawful detentions during the reporting period.

Role of the Police and Security Apparatus

The Ministry of Defense oversees both the Fiji Police Force and the Republic of Fiji Military Force (RFMF). Police are responsible for law enforcement and the maintenance of internal security. The RFMF is responsible for external security. The POAD also authorizes soldiers to perform the duties and functions of police and prison officers in specific circumstances.

The police Ethical Standards Unit is responsible for investigating complaints of police misconduct. On July 28, the Fiji Police reported a 2 percent reduction in complaints and disciplinary offenses by officers. According to police, most complaints related to the criminal investigation process. The Fiji Independent Commission against Corruption (FICAC) investigated public agencies and officials, including some members of police and military forces. As of May, six police and military members appeared in court on bribery-related charges. On August 2, a court sentenced a senior police officer to 12 months in jail for criminal intimidation and assault occasioning actual bodily harm. Impunity and corruption remained problems, however.

In an attempt to increase respect for human rights by security forces, the FHRADC, international organizations, and local nongovernmental organizations (NGOs) conducted a number of human rights training courses with law enforcers.

The constitution and POAD provide immunity from prosecution for members of the security forces for any deaths or injuries arising from the use of force deemed necessary to enforce public order. Legal proceedings for five security force officers charged in 2015 for the alleged sexual assault on an escaped prisoner, Ioane Benedito, in 2012 remains pending.

The constitution provides immunity for the president, prime minister, members of the cabinet, and security forces for actions taken relating to the 2006 coup, the 2009 abrogation of the 1997 constitution, and the suppression of a mutiny at military headquarters in 2000.

Arrest Procedures and Treatment of Detainees

The constitution provides that detained persons be charged and produced in court within 48 hours of arrest or as soon as practicable thereafter. Police officers may arrest persons without a warrant for violations of the crimes decree. On July 21, four of the men apprehended and charged for the unlawful cultivation of marijuana during a joint police raid in June were released on bail (pending trial) approximately 21 days after police initially detained them.

Police also arrest persons in response to warrants issued by magistrates and judges. Police may detain persons under the POAD for a maximum of 16 days, at which point authorities must charge or release persons in custody. There is no legal requirement to produce persons detained under provisions of the POAD in court for judicial review of the grounds for their detention, unless authorities charge them with an offense. The POAD prohibits any court, tribunal, or other body from reviewing a detention under POAD provisions.

The law gives accused persons the right to bail, unless it is "not in the interests of justice" to grant bail. Under the law both police and the courts may grant bail. There is a presumption in favor of granting bail, although the prosecution may object, as often happened in cases where the accused was appealing a conviction or had previously breached bail conditions. An individual must apply for bail by a motion and affidavit that require the services of a lawyer.

Authorities generally allowed detainees prompt access to counsel and family members. The Legal Aid Commission provided counsel to some indigent defendants in criminal cases, a service supplemented by voluntary services from private attorneys. There were delays in the provision of legal aid to some accused persons due to lack of adequate legal aid staff and resources. On November 2, the Fiji Police Force launched a six-month "First Hour Procedure" and digital recording pilot project at the central police station (Totogo) in Suva. As a part of the project, police are expected to provide every suspect with legal aid assistance within the first hour of arrest. In addition police are required to record the "caution interview" with each suspect before questioning, to confirm that police inform all suspects of their constitutional rights and to confirm whether suspects have suffered any abuse by police prior to questioning.

<u>Pretrial Detention</u>: During the year the number of pretrial detainees remained high because of a continuing pattern of refusal of bail by the courts. In 2014 pretrial detainees made up approximately 24 per cent of the prison population. A shortage of prosecutors and judges contributed to slow processing of cases. Consequently, some defendants faced lengthy pretrial detention.

<u>Detainee's Ability to Challenge Lawfulness of Detention before a Court</u>: The bill of rights grants detained persons the right to "challenge the lawfulness of the detention in person before a court and, if the detention is unlawful, to be released." Persons found to have been detained unlawfully may seek compensation through domestic courts.

e. Denial of Fair Public Trial

The constitution provides for an independent judiciary subject only to the constitution and law but gives the president, prime minister, and attorney general control over the appointment and removal of the chief justice and other members of the judiciary. The president appoints or removes from office the judges of the Supreme Court, justices of appeal, and judges of the High Court on the recommendation of the Judicial Service Commission in consultation with the attorney general. The commission, following consultations with the attorney general, may appoint magistrates, masters of the High Court, the chief registrar, and other judicial officers. The constitution and various decrees provide for a variety of restrictions on the jurisdiction of the courts.

An amended decree removed the courts' jurisdiction to hear challenges to government decisions on judicial restructuring, terms and conditions of remuneration for the judiciary, and terminated court cases. Various other decrees contained similar clauses limiting the jurisdiction of the courts on decisions made by cabinet, ministers, or government departments.

Trial Procedures

In most cases defendants have the right to a fair public trial, and the court system generally enforced this right during the year.

The crimes decree defines which offenses may be tried in the magistrates' courts and which must be tried in the High Court. The magistrates' courts heard most cases. Only the High Court may hear serious offenses, including murder, rape, trafficking in persons, bribery, treason, sedition, and mutiny. Defendants enjoy a presumption of innocence; they may not be compelled to testify or confess guilt. They may present witnesses and evidence on their own behalf, confront witnesses against them, and access government-held evidence relevant to their cases. Defendants have the right to be informed promptly and in detail of the charges against them, with free interpretation if necessary through all appeals. Authorities also must accord them adequate time and facilities to prepare a defense and be present at trial. In most cases defendants have the right to counsel, but many were unaware of their rights when detained or interviewed and, therefore, often did not ask for legal counsel. The Legal Aid Commission, supplemented by voluntary services of private attorneys, provided free counsel to some indigent defendants in criminal cases. The right of appeal exists, but delays in the process often hampered this right. All citizens receive these rights without discrimination.

Political Prisoners and Detainees

There were no reports of political prisoners or detainees.

Civil Judicial Procedures and Remedies

Individuals and organizations may seek civil remedies for human rights violations through domestic courts. In the event of a human rights violation, an individual may complain to the FHRADC, but the constitution prohibits FHRADC from investigating cases filed by individuals and organizations relating to the 2006 coup and the 2009 abrogation of the previous constitution.

f. Arbitrary or Unlawful Interference with Privacy, Family, Home, or Correspondence

The POAD permits military personnel to search persons and premises without a warrant from a court and to take photographs, fingerprints, and measurements of any person. Police and military officers also may enter private premises to break up any meeting considered unlawful. There were no credible reports police did so during the year.

Section 2. Respect for Civil Liberties, Including:

a. Freedom of Speech and Press

The constitution provides for freedom of expression, speech, thought, opinion, and publication, but it grants the government authority to restrict these rights for a broad array of reasons. These include preventing hate speech and insurrection; maintaining national security, public order, public safety, public morality, public health, and the orderly conduct of elections; protecting the reputation, privacy, dignity, and rights of other persons; and enforcing media standards and regulating the conduct of media organizations. Additionally, the POAD gives the government power to detain persons on suspicion of "endangering public safety" and to "preserve the peace." The Media Industry Development Decree prohibits "irresponsible reporting" and provides for government censorship of media.

<u>Freedom of Speech and Expression</u>: The crimes decree includes criticism of the government in its definition of the crime of sedition. This includes statements made in other countries by any person, who authorities may prosecute on their return to the country. The courts set the trial for more than 60 defendants in an August 2015 sedition case for 2017. The government charged the defendants for seditious acts in 2015 following claims of military-style training and an attempt to establish a breakaway state on the main island of Viti Levu.

The POAD defines as terrorism any act designed to advance a political, religious, or ideological cause that could "reasonably be regarded" as intended to compel a government to do or refrain from doing any act or to intimidate the public or a section thereof. It also makes acts of religious vilification and attempts to sabotage or undermine the country's economy offenses punishable by a maximum 10,000 Fijian dollars (F\$) (\$4,870) fine or five years in prison.

The 2015 Flag Protection Act makes any use of Fiji's flag to "demean, disrespect, or insult the State, the Government or any member of Government, or the general public" an offense punishable by up to 10 years' imprisonment and a fine of F\$20,000 (\$9,750). According to the law, "the onus of proof shall be on the Defendant to prove his or her innocence."

<u>Press and Media Freedoms</u>: Independent media were active and expressed a wide variety of views without restriction, despite the media decree and monitoring by the Media Industry Development Authority (MIDA).

Public debate improved markedly as news media published a more diverse range of political commentary.

The government continued to publish fortnightly supplements and most of its advertisements in the *Fiji Sun* newspaper, which was generally progovernment.

<u>Violence and Harassment</u>: On August 17, the Office of the Director of Public Prosecutions (ODPP) charged three media agency staff and the author of a letter to the editor for allegedly breaching the crimes decree, which prohibits any communication that promotes "feelings of enmity or ill-will between different communities, religious groups or classes of the community." The ODPP charged the four men for inciting communal antagonism against the Muslim community with an article published on April 27 in the *Fiji Times* indigenous-language newspaper, *Nai Lalakai*. The maximum penalty for the offense is 10 years' imprisonment. The four defendants in the case were *Fiji Times* Editor in Chief Fred Wesley, *Fiji Times* General Manager Hank Arts, journalist Anare Ravula, and letter author Josaia Waqabaca.

<u>Censorship or Content Restrictions</u>: The media decree contains a provision authorizing the Ministry of Information to censor all news stories before broadcast or publication. Although the government ceased formal media censorship under the decree in 2012, journalists and media organizations continued to practice varying degrees of self-censorship. Media published opinion articles by academics and commentators perceived as antigovernment.

Under the media decree, the directors and 90 percent of the shareholders of locally based media must be citizens of, and permanently resident in, the country. MIDA is responsible for enforcing these provisions and has the power to investigate journalists and media outlets for alleged violations of the decree, including powers of search and seizure of equipment. The decree established a media tribunal to decide complaints referred by the authority, with the power to impose fines of up to F$25,000 ($12,200) for publishers and editors, and F$100,000 ($48,700) for media organizations. In contrast to previous years, amendments to the media decree removed jail terms of up to two years and fines of up to F$1,000 ($487) for journalists. The tribunal, which consists of a single judge, is not bound by formal rules of evidence. The decree strips the judiciary of power to review the decree or any proceedings or findings of MIDA, the tribunal, or the information minister.

The code of ethics in the media decree requires that media publish balanced material. It obligates media to give any individual or organization an opportunity to reply to comments or materials for publication. Journalists reported that this requirement did not restrict reporting as much as in years past but said self-censorship continued to be a problem.

The television amendment decree requires television license holders to operate in conformance with the media decree's code of ethics.

Libel/Slander Laws: The constitution includes the need to protect the reputation of persons as allowable limitations to freedom of expression. The threat of prosecution for contempt of court or under provisions of the media decree and the POAD was sufficient incentive for media to continue to practice self-censorship.

National Security: The constitution includes national security as an allowable limitation to freedom of expression. While the threat of prosecution for contempt of court or under provisions of the media decree and the POAD was sufficient incentive to media to practice self-censorship, some media outlets have begun to report on issues previously considered too sensitive for publication.

Actions to Expand Press Freedom: In October the government lifted all remaining bans on foreign journalists seeking to enter the country, including the bans on New Zealand journalists Michael Field and Barbara Dreaver, and Australian journalist Sean Dorney.

Internet Freedom

The government did not restrict or disrupt access to the internet or censor online content, and there were no credible reports that the government monitored private online communications without legal authority. By decree all telephone and internet service users must register their personal details with telephone and internet providers, including name, birth date, home address, left thumbprint, and photographic identification. The decree imposes fines of up to F$100,000 ($48,700) on providers who continued to provide services to unregistered users and up to F$10,000 ($4,870) on users who did not update their registration information as required.

The internet was widely available and used in and around urban centers, but its availability and use were minimal or nonexistent outside urban areas.

Academic Freedom and Cultural Events

The constitution provides for academic freedom, although contract regulations of the University of the South Pacific effectively restricted most university employees from running for or holding public office or holding an official position with any political party. Persons entering the country on tourist visas wishing to conduct research must notify and seek permission of the government.

b. Freedom of Peaceful Assembly and Association

The constitution provides for the freedoms of assembly and association, but with restrictions.

Freedom of Assembly

The constitution provides for freedom of assembly but allows the government to limit this right in the interests of national security, public safety, public order, public morality, public health, and the orderly conduct of elections. The constitution also allows the government to limit freedom of assembly to protect the rights of others and imposes restrictions on a public official's right to freedom of assembly.

The POAD allows the government to refuse permit applications for any meeting or march deemed to prejudice peace, public safety, and good order or to sabotage or attempt to undermine the economy. It also allows authorities to use whatever force is deemed necessary to prohibit or disperse public and private meetings after "due warning" to preserve public order.

According to the ODPP, on September 10 and 11, police detained opposition National Federation Party (NFP) Leader Dr. Biman Prasad, opposition Social Liberal Democratic Party (SODELPA) Leader Sitiveni Rabuka, Fiji Islands Council of Trade Unions Leader Attar Singh, former SODELPA politician and academic Dr. Tupeni Baba, Director of the NGO Pacific Dialogue Jone Dakuvula, and Fiji Labor Party Leader Mahendra Chaudhry "on suspicion of having breached the Public Order Act 1969 (as amended)" by attending a public meeting that had not been permitted by police.

On October 17, the ODPP dropped the charges, citing "insufficient evidence to sustain a charge for a breach of the Public Order Act in so far as there was no intention on the part of these persons to attend the meeting in breach of the Act." The ODPP also noted that there was insufficient evidence for charges of incitement and that the arrests "appeared selective."

Although event organizers said that the permitting process was sometimes very slow, authorities granted permits for public rallies in support of West Papuan independence, UN Human Rights Day, and the 16 Days of Activism against Domestic Violence Campaign.

Freedom of Association

The constitution provides for freedom of association but limits this right in the interests of national security, public order, and morality and also for the orderly conduct of elections. It allows the government to regulate trade unions and collective bargaining processes, strikes and lockouts, and essential industries in the interests of the economy and the population. On February 15, Fiji's Employment Relations (Amendment) Act 2016 came into force, providing for the right for all workers to join trade or enterprise unions. The government generally did not restrict membership in other NGOs, professional associations, and other private organizations.

c. Freedom of Religion

See the Department of State's *International Religious Freedom Report* at www.state.gov/religiousfreedomreport/.

d. Freedom of Movement, Internally Displaced Persons, Protection of Refugees, and Stateless Persons

Under the POAD, the government may restrict freedom of internal movement, foreign travel, emigration, and repatriation.

The government cooperated with the Office of the UN High Commissioner for Refugees and other humanitarian organizations in providing protection and assistance to internally displaced persons, refugees, returning refugees, asylum seekers, stateless persons, and other persons of concern.

In-country Movement: The POAD authorizes the government to prohibit, restrict, or regulate movement of persons, but the government did not restrict any person's in-country movement during the year.

Exile: Opposition parties called on the government to lift travel bans on all existing and former Fiji citizens, including former Fiji citizen and academic Brij

Lal. The Immigration Department has stated that Dr. Lal may reapply for re-entry into Fiji.

Protection of Refugees

<u>Access to Asylum</u>: The law provides for the granting of asylum or refugee status, and the government has established a system for providing protection to refugees.

Section 3. Freedom to Participate in the Political Process

The constitution and electoral decree provide citizens the ability to choose their government in free and fair periodic elections generally held by secret ballot and based on universal and equal suffrage. In the 2014 election, voters with disabilities and in need of assistance were required to rely on the assistance of an electoral official in order to vote.

Elections and Political Participation

<u>Recent Elections</u>: In 2014 voters elected 50 members of parliament. The Fiji First party won 32 seats and an outright majority, and Josaia Voreqe (Frank) Bainimarama was sworn in as prime minister. Observers deemed the elections generally credible and "broadly reflected the will of the Fijian people."

<u>Political Parties and Political Participation</u>: The constitution provides for the right to form and join political parties, to campaign for political parties or a cause, to register as a voter, to vote by secret ballot in elections or referendums, to run for public office, and to hold that office. These rights are limited, however, to allow the government to prescribe eligibility requirements for voters, candidates, political party officials, and holders of public office.

Under the POAD, permits are required for political meetings in both public and private venues.

The Political Parties Registration Decree requires that parties submit applications, which must include 5,000 member signatures, for registration. Only three parties, two independent candidates, and four newly formed parties have registered successfully since 2013. No new parties registered during the year. The law allows deregistration of political parties for any election offense and mandates trade union leaders must quit their positions before running as candidates.

The Electoral Decree restricts any person, entity, or organization receiving funding from foreign governments, intergovernmental or NGOs, or multilateral agencies from conducting or participating in any campaigns, including meetings, debates, panel discussions, interviews, publishing materials, or any public forum discussing the elections. Convictions for violations of the decree incur up to 10 years in prison, a F$50,000 ($24,400) fine, or both. The decree allows universities to hold panel discussions and organize inclusive public forums.

On February 1, the supervisor of elections suspended the three-member opposition party NFP over an auditing infringement relating to the party's financial accounts. The suspension effectively barred the members from parliament for 30 days as well as prevented them from operating and functioning as a political party. On February 15, the NFP filed court proceedings challenging the decision. The party also sought legal advice on whether the speaker acted correctly in her decision to suspend the lawmakers from parliament.

The Fijian Elections Office lifted the suspension on February 18, after the auditing infringements were addressed. The NFP continued legal action in court for a determination concerning the legality of the suspension.

On May 11, government members of the Public Accounts Committee (PAC) voted out PAC Chair Biman Prasad, who was also the leader of the opposition party NFP. The PAC is responsible for scrutinizing the government's financial accounts. The removal of the chair follows government changes to parliament's standing orders on February 11, which removed a long-standing requirement for a member of the opposition to chair the PAC. With three of the five seats on the PAC, the government was able to elect one of its members, Ashneel Sudhakar, as the committee's new chair.

Other amendments to the standing orders also reduced the opposition's power and ability to introduce petitions in parliament. Any petition tabled in parliament requires the support of at least 20 parliamentarians (40 percent) before members may present it for debate in parliament.

On June 3, female opposition parliamentarian Tupou Draunidalo was suspended from parliament for calling a government minister "a fool" while responding to comments about opposition members of parliament. Under the terms of the suspension, Draunidalo would not be able to sit in parliament for the remainder of her two-year term. On September 29, male opposition parliamentarian Ratu Isoa Tikoca was similarly sanctioned for the remainder of his two-year term for comments he made on July 6, listing Muslim officials serving in high government office.

<u>Participation of Women and Minorities</u>: Cultural beliefs restricted participation of most indigenous women in political life. Indo-Fijians, who accounted for 36 percent of the population, continued to be underrepresented at senior levels of the military. Indo-Fijians comprised approximately 35 percent of the civil service overall and approximately one-third of the police force; observers estimated the military and prison services to be more than 95 percent indigenous Fijian.

Section 4. Corruption and Lack of Transparency in Government

The law provides criminal penalties for corruption by officials, but the government did not implement the law effectively, and officials sometimes engaged in corrupt practices with impunity. There were numerous reports of government corruption during the year.

<u>Corruption</u>: Measures by the government during the year to combat corruption within the bureaucracy, including FICAC public service announcements encouraging citizens to report corrupt government activities, had some effect on systemic corruption. In May former corrections chief Lieutenant Colonel Ifereimi Vasu, who the government dismissed in December 2015 for abuse of office charges in relation to a prison mini-mart, reappeared in court. The case against Vasu continued at year's end.

Media published articles on FICAC investigations on abuse of office, and anonymous blogs reported on some government corruption. Since 2008, in the absence of a sitting parliament, the auditor general had submitted audit reports to the cabinet. The cabinet referred such reports to the Public Accounts Committee for review but did not make them public. The auditor general's reports from 2007 to 2013 that were tabled in parliament were made publicly available during the year.

On May 29, reports indicated that the Office of the Director of Public Prosecutions investigated 17 individuals for alleged abuse of cyclone relief funds and charged six of them for this offense.

On August 19, a clerk in the Ministry of Finance received a sentence of four years in prison after he was found guilty of abuse of office.

<u>Financial Disclosure</u>: There are no laws requiring income and asset disclosure by appointed or elected officials. FICAC reports directly to the attorney general and is the primary body responsible for combating and prosecuting government corruption. The government adequately funded FICAC, but some observers questioned its independence and viewed some of its high-profile prosecutions as politically motivated, such as an April 2015 case against opposition parliamentarian Ratu Isoa Tikoca for failure to declare liabilities under the political parties' decree, which requires disclosures by candidates standing for election and party officials.

<u>Public Access to Information</u>: The constitution provides for public access to government information and for the correction or deletion of false or misleading information that affects any person. The constitution requires that the government enact a freedom of information law and circulate draft legislation for public comment in October, but parliament had not tabled the legislation at year's end. The government sometimes was unresponsive to public requests for information.

Section 5. Governmental Attitude Regarding International and Nongovernmental Investigation of Alleged Violations of Human Rights

A variety of domestic and international human rights groups generally operated without government restriction, investigating and publishing their findings on human rights cases. Government officials were somewhat cooperative and responsive to their views.

NGO operations were constrained by the crimes decree, which includes criticism of the government in its definition of sedition; the POAD, which contains a broad prohibition on speech that could damage the economy; and the media decree, which authorizes the government to regulate media content.

<u>Government Human Rights Bodies</u>: The constitution establishes the FHRADC as the successor to the Fiji Human Rights Commission, but, like its predecessor, the law prohibits the FHRADC from investigating cases filed by individuals and organizations relating to the 2006 coup and the 2009 abrogation of the previous constitution. On March 16, after a lapse of seven years, the FHRADC announced the appointment of MIDA chair Ashwin Raj as the commission's new director. Local critics pointed out that Raj's role as MIDA chair and links to the previous military government could be a cause for conflict of interest. The commission received a 70 percent increase in the 2016 national budget.

The FHRADC continued to receive reports of human rights violations lodged by citizens. On July 6, the FHRADC reportedly assisted with the case of young male who alleged police brutalized him when he was taken in as a suspect for a crime. On August 10, the FHRADC confirmed that since 2013, the commission had received 703 complaints of human rights violations.

Section 6. Discrimination, Societal Abuses, and Trafficking in Persons

Women

Rape and Domestic Violence: Rape, domestic abuse, incest, and indecent assault were significant problems. The law provides for a maximum punishment of life imprisonment for rape, an indictable offense that only the High Court may try. The law recognizes spousal rape as a specific offense. The NGOs Fiji Women's Rights Movement and Fiji Women's Crisis Center pressed for more consistent and severe punishment for rape.

The domestic violence decree identifies domestic violence as a specific offense. Police enforced the practice of a "no-drop" policy, whereby they pursued investigations of domestic violence cases even if a victim later withdrew the accusation. Women's organizations reported police were not always consistent in their observance of this policy. The decree gives police authority to apply to a magistrate for restraining orders in domestic violence cases, but police often told victims to apply for such orders themselves. Police officers were not always aware they had the power to apply on the victim's behalf, and complainants sometimes were obliged to seek legal assistance from a lawyer or NGO. Courts dismissed some cases of domestic abuse and incest or gave perpetrators light sentences. Traditional and religious practices of reconciliation between aggrieved parties in both indigenous and Indo-Fijian communities were sometimes taken into account to mitigate sentences in domestic violence cases, although Police Commissioner Sitiveni Qiliho said that police would continue to charge the sexual offenders regardless of such practices. In some cases offenders were released without a conviction rather than jailed on the condition they maintain good behavior. Several locally based NGOs sought to raise public awareness of domestic violence.

Four women's crisis centers funded by foreign governments operated in the country. The centers offered counseling and assistance to women in cases of domestic violence, rape, and other problems, such as a lack of child support.

<u>Sexual Harassment</u>: A decree prohibits sexual harassment, and the government used criminal law against "indecent assaults on females," which prohibit offending the modesty of women, to prosecute sexual harassment cases. Under the Employment Relations law, workers may file complaints on the ground of sexual harassment in the workplace.

<u>Reproductive Rights</u>: Couples and individuals generally have the right to decide the number, spacing, and timing of their children; to have the information and means to do so; and to manage their reproductive health, free from discrimination, coercion, and violence. According to UN Population Division estimates, 43 percent of women of reproductive age used a modern method of contraception in 2015. The government provided family planning services, and women had access to contraceptives free of charge at public hospitals and clinics, and for a nominal fee if prescribed by a private physician. Nevertheless, NGOs reported some women faced societal and family pressure against obtaining contraceptives. Unmarried and young women generally were discouraged from undergoing tubal ligation for birth control, and public hospitals, especially in rural areas, often refused to perform the operation on unmarried women who requested it. Nurses and doctors often required the husband's consent before operating on a married woman, although there is no legal requirement for such consent. Most women gave birth in hospitals, where skilled health attendants and essential prenatal, obstetric, and postpartum care were available.

<u>Discrimination</u>: Women have full rights of inheritance and property ownership by law, but local authorities often excluded them from the decision-making process on disposition of indigenous communal land, which constituted more than 80 percent of all land. Women have the right to a share in the distribution of indigenous land lease proceeds, but authorities seldom recognized this right. Women have the same rights and status as men under family law and in the judicial system. Nonetheless, women and children had difficulties having protection orders enforced by police in domestic violence cases.

Although the law prohibits discrimination based on gender and requires equal pay for equal work, employers generally paid women less than men for similar work (see section 7.d.). Several prominent women led civil society, NGO, and advocacy groups.

The Ministry for Women, Social Welfare, and Poverty Alleviation worked to promote women's legal rights.

Children

<u>Birth Registration</u>: Citizenship is derived both from birth within the country and through one's parents. Parents were generally able to register births promptly.

<u>Child Abuse</u>: Corporal punishment was common in both homes and schools, despite a Ministry of Education policy forbidding it in the classroom. Increasing urbanization, overcrowding, and the breakdown of traditional community and extended-family-based structures put children at risk for abuse and appeared to be factors that contributed to a child's chance of exploitation for commercial sex.

<u>Early and Forced Marriage</u>: The legal minimum age for marriage is 18. Some NGOs reported that, especially in rural areas, girls often married at age 18, preventing them from completing their secondary school education. In indigenous villages, girls under age 18 who became pregnant could live as common-law wives with their child's father after the men presented traditional apologies to the girls' families, thereby avoiding the filing of a complaint to police by the families. The girls frequently married the fathers as soon as legally permissible.

<u>Sexual Exploitation of Children</u>: Commercial sexual exploitation of children continued to occur. It is an offense for any person to buy or hire a child under age 18 for sex, exploitation in prostitution, or other unlawful purpose; the offense is punishable by imprisonment for up to 12 years. Commercial sexual exploitation of children is an indictable offense that the High Court must try. No prosecutions or convictions for trafficking of children occurred during the year.

It is an offense for a householder or innkeeper to allow commercial sexual exploitation of children in his or her premises, but there were no known prosecutions or convictions for such offenses during the year.

Some high school age children and homeless and jobless youth engaged in prostitution during the year, and there were reported cases of child sex tourism in tourist centers, such as Nadi and Savusavu. In some cases taxi drivers, hoteliers, bar workers, and others reportedly acted as intermediaries facilitating the commercial sexual exploitation of children. Family members, other Fijian citizens, foreign tourists, and crewmembers on foreign fishing vessels also reportedly participated in the prostitution of Fijian children.

The minimum age for consensual sex is 16. The Court of Appeal has ruled that 10 years is the minimum appropriate sentence in child rape cases, but, in such cases, police often charged defendants with "defilement" rather than rape because defilement is easier to prove in court. Defilement or unlawful carnal knowledge of a child under age 13 has a maximum penalty of life imprisonment, while the maximum penalty for defilement of a child between ages 13 and 15, or of a person with intellectual disabilities, is 10 years in prison.

Child pornography is illegal. The maximum penalty for violators is 14 years in prison, a maximum fine of F$25,000 ($12,200), or both for a first offense and life imprisonment, a fine of up to F$50,000 ($24,400), or both for a repeat offense, and the confiscation of any equipment used in the commission of the offense.

The child welfare decree requires mandatory reporting to police by teachers and health and social welfare workers of any incident of child abuse.

International Child Abductions: The country is a party to the 1980 Hague Convention on the Civil Aspects of International Child Abduction. See the Department of State's *Annual Report on International Parental Child Abduction* at travel.state.gov/content/childabduction/en/legal/compliance.html.

Anti-Semitism

There was a small Jewish community composed mainly of foreign residents. There were no reports of anti-Semitic acts.

Trafficking in Persons

See the Department of State's *Trafficking in Persons Report* at www.state.gov/j/tip/rls/tiprpt/.

Persons with Disabilities

The constitution considers all persons equal, and discrimination against persons with disabilities in employment, education, provision of housing and land, or provision of other state services is illegal. Statutes provide for the right of access to places and all modes of transport generally open to the public. The constitution addresses specifically the right of persons with disabilities to reasonable access to all places, public transport, and information, as well as the right to use Braille or sign language and to reasonable access to materials and devices relating to the disability; the law, however, does not further define "reasonable." Additionally, the constitution provides that the law may limit these rights "as necessary." Public health regulations provide penalties for noncompliance, but there was very little enabling legislation on accessibility for persons with disabilities, and there was little or no enforcement of laws protecting them.

Building regulations require new public buildings to be accessible to persons with disabilities, but only a few existing buildings met this requirement. By law all new office spaces must be accessible to persons with disabilities. There were only a small number of vehicles in the country accessible to persons with disabilities. Persons with disabilities continued to face employment discrimination (see section 7.d.). There were no government programs to improve access to information and communications for persons with disabilities, and persons with disabilities, in particular those with hearing or vision disabilities, had difficulty accessing public information. Government employed a sign-language interpreter to provide translation service on nationwide television during the national budget address in parliament. A number of community organizations assisted persons with disabilities, particularly children.

There were a number of separate schools offering primary education for persons with physical, intellectual, and sensory disabilities; however, cost and location limited access. Some students attended mainstream primary schools, and the Early Intervention Center monitored them. Opportunities for a secondary school or higher education for persons with disabilities was very limited.

A decree stipulates that the community, public health, and general health systems should provide treatment for persons with mental and intellectual disabilities in the community, public health, and general health systems. Society, however, separated most persons with such disabilities, and their families supported them at home. Institutionalization of persons with more significant mental disabilities was in a single, underfunded public facility in Suva.

On August 30, the Fijian Elections Office signed terms of reference with the Pacific Disability Forum and the Fiji National Council for Disabled Persons to create an Elections Disability Access Working Group to improve the political participation of the country's disability community. The national council, a government-funded statutory body, worked to protect the rights of persons with disabilities. Several NGOs also promoted attention to the needs of persons with various disabilities.

National/Racial/Ethnic Minorities

Tension between indigenous Fijians and the Indo-Fijian minority is a longstanding problem. Indigenous Fijians make up an estimated 58 percent of the population, Indo-Fijians comprise 36 percent, and the remaining 6 percent is composed of Europeans, Chinese, Rotuman, and other Pacific Islander communities. The abrogated constitution contained a nonjusticiable compact that cited the "paramountcy" of Fijian interests as a guiding principle and provided for affirmative action and "social justice" programs to "secure effective equality" for ethnic Fijians and Rotumans as well as for other communities. The compact chiefly benefited the indigenous Fijian majority, although Indo-Fijians dominated the commercial sector. The government publicly stated its opposition to such policies, which it characterized as racist, and called for the elimination of discriminatory laws and practices that favor one race over another. Indigenous Fijians continued to dominate the security forces.

Land tenure remained a highly sensitive and politicized issue. Indigenous Fijians communally held approximately 87 percent of all land, the government held 4 percent, and the remainder was freehold land, which private individuals or companies held. The iTaukei Land Trust Board holds all indigenous land in a statutory trust for the benefit of indigenous landholding units.

Most cash-crop farmers were Indo-Fijians, the majority of whom are descendants of indentured laborers who came to the country during the British colonial era. Virtually all Indo-Fijian farmers must lease land from ethnic Fijian landowners. Many Indo-Fijians believed that limits on their ability to own land and their consequent dependency on leased land from indigenous Fijians constituted de facto discrimination against them. Many indigenous Fijian landowners believed that the rental formulas prescribed in the national land tenure legislation discriminated against them as the resource owners. This situation contributed significantly to communal tensions.

By law all indigenous Fijians are automatically registered upon birth into an official Fijian register of native landowners known as the *Vola ni Kawa Bula* (or native land register). The register also verifies access for those in it to indigenous communally owned lands and justifies titleholders within indigenous communities.

Acts of Violence, Discrimination, and Other Abuses Based on Sexual Orientation and Gender Identity

The constitution prohibits discrimination on the grounds of sexual orientation, gender, and gender identity and expression. The Employment Relations law prohibits discrimination in employment based on sexual orientation.

There was some societal discrimination against persons based on sexual orientation and gender identity, although there was no systemic discrimination. On January 6, Prime Minister Bainimarama said that for as long as his tenure in government leadership continued, there would be no same-sex marriage in the country. After some from the community voiced fears of backlash because of the prime minister's remarks, Police Commissioner Sitiveni Qiliho assured the lesbian, gay, bisexual, transgender, and intersex (LGBTI) community that police would protect the LGBTI community in line with the bill of rights in the constitution.

The FHRADC reported complaints of discrimination against LGBTI persons in such areas as employment, housing, or access to health care.

While some with deeply held religious beliefs found same-sex sexual conduct objectionable, in general attitudes toward LGBTI individuals continued to become more accepting. In May various communities held events to promote and celebrate the equal rights of LGBTI persons such as the International Day against Homophobia, Transphobia, and Biphobia.

HIV and AIDS Social Stigma

There was some societal discrimination against persons with HIV/AIDS, although it was not systemic. There were no known cases of violence targeting persons with HIV/AIDS.

Section 7. Worker Rights

a. Freedom of Association and the Right to Collective Bargaining

On February 15, the Employment Relations (Amendment) Act of 2016 entered into force. The law expands reforms introduced by the Employment Relations Act of 2015 following the joint report issued by the Fiji Commerce and Employers Federation, the government, and the Fiji Trades Union Congress (FTUC) on January 29. The new law provides all workers the right to form and join independent unions, bargain collectively, and strike. The 2016 act also reinstated any employment dispute terminated under the Essential National Industries Decree

(ENID, repealed in 2015). As of October 17, 186 individual worker disputes terminated under the ENID had been referred to Arbitration Court.

The law prohibits some forms of antiunion discrimination, including victimizing workers or firing a worker for belonging to a union. The constitution prohibits union officers from becoming members of parliament. The Political Parties Decree also limits the ability of union officers to form or join political parties and exercise other political rights.

The law designates "essential service and industries" to include the 11 corporations in eight sectors specified in the 2011 Essential Industries Decree: finance, telecommunications, public sector employees, and the airline industry. The 2015 Employment Relations Amendment Act extended the definition of essential services and industries to include also all state-owned enterprises, statutory authorities, and local government authorities.

The law also limits who is able to be an officer of a trade union, including prohibiting noncitizens from being trade union officers.

All unions must register with the government, which has discretionary power to refuse to register any union with an "undesirable" name, although the 2016 act limits the government's discretion to refuse to register trade union names to those cases where the name is "offensive, or racially or ethnically discriminatory." The government may cancel registration of existing unions in exceptional cases provided for by law.

By law any trade union with seven or more members that is not in an industry designated as essential may enter into collective bargaining with an employer.

Unions may conduct secret strike ballots upon 14 days' notice to the registrar if 50 percent of all members who are entitled to vote approve the strike. Workers in essential services may strike but must also give 14 days' notice, notify the Arbitration Court, and provide the category of workers who propose to strike and the starting date and location of the strike. The law permits the minister of employment to declare a strike unlawful and refer the dispute to the Arbitration Court. If authorities refer the issue to the court, workers and strike leaders could face criminal charges if they persist in strike action.

Limited data were available on the government's enforcement of new legal provisions on freedom of association and collective bargaining. Penalties under law for violations of freedom of association and collective bargaining included fines and imprisonment; observers considered them sufficient to deter violations. Individuals, employers, and unions (on behalf of their members) may submit employment disputes and grievances alleging discrimination, unfair dismissal, sexual harassment, or certain other unfair labor practices to the Ministry of Employment, Productivity, and Industrial Relations.

The two trade union umbrella bodies, the FTUC and the Fiji Islands Council of Trade Unions, were able to hold meetings during the year and operate without government interference.

On March 24, in coordination with labor union leaders and employers, the government amended labor laws to guarantee that workers have freedom of association and the right to organize. As a result, the International Labor Organization Governing Body agreed to close the Article 26 complaint, filed in 2013, and did not pursue a Commission of Inquiry. Several problems remain, and the ILO has agreed to provide technical assistance to help resolve them.

b. Prohibition of Forced or Compulsory Labor

The constitution and the law prohibit all forms of forced or compulsory labor.

The Labor Inspectorate, police, and Department of Immigration are responsible for enforcing the law, depending on the circumstances of the particular case. The law prescribes penalties of up to 25 years in prison, which observers generally considered sufficient to deter violations.

There were reports that forced labor occurred, including forced labor of children (see section 7.c.). The government effectively enforced the law.

Also see the Department of State's *Trafficking in Persons Report* at www.state.gov/j/tip/rls/tiprpt/.

c. Prohibition of Child Labor and Minimum Age for Employment

Children under age 12 may not work except in a family-owned business or agricultural enterprise. Any such employment must not interfere with school attendance and is to be of limited duration. Although the law provides that education is compulsory until age 15, children between ages 13 and 15 may be employed on a daily wage basis in nonindustrial "light" work not involving machinery, provided they return to their parents or guardian every night. The law does not limit, however, the number of hours children may engage in light work, nor does it include a list of activities that are permissible. Children between the ages 15 and 17 may be employed, but they must be given specified hours and rest breaks. They may not be employed in hazardous occupations and activities, including those involving heavy machinery, hazardous materials, mining, or heavy physical labor.

The Ministry of Employment deployed inspectors nationwide to enforce compliance with labor laws, including those covering child labor. The government effectively enforced applicable laws, and penalties were generally sufficient to deter violations. The law provides for imprisonment of up to two years, fines of up to F$50,000 ($24,400), or both, for companies who violate these provisions. During the year the Interagency Committee on Child Labor, a multiagency task force led by the Ministry of Employment, continued to work with NGOs and labor organizations to implement programs through the ILO's Tackling Child Labor through Education program.

Poverty continued to lead children to migrate to urban areas for work, increasing their vulnerability to exploitation, and to work as casual laborers, often with no safeguards against abuse or injury. Child labor continued in the informal sector and in hazardous work, including work as wheelbarrow boys and casual laborers, including in cane farming and other agriculture. Commercial sexual exploitation of children occurred (see section 6). Some children working in the homes of relatives were vulnerable to involuntary domestic servitude or forced to engage in sexual activity in exchange for food, clothing, shelter, or school fees.

Also see the Department of Labor's *Findings on the Worst Forms of Child Labor* at www.dol.gov/ilab/reports/child-labor/findings.

d. Discrimination with Respect to Employment and Occupation

The 2007 Employment Promulgation prohibits employment discrimination based on ethnic origin, color, place of origin, gender, sexual orientation, birth, primary language, economic status, age, disability, HIV/AIDS status, social class, marital status, employment status, family status, opinion, religion, or belief. The 2016 act expanded the scope of legal prohibitions against employment discrimination to bar discrimination based on race, social origin, gender identity or expression, health status, conscience, or pregnancy. The law stipulates that every employer shall pay male and female workers equal remuneration for work of equal value. The law prohibits women working underground in mines but places no other legal limitations on the employment of women.

Limited data were available on the government's antidiscrimination provisions. Penalties for employment discrimination included fines and imprisonment and were generally sufficient to deter violations.

Discrimination in employment and wages occurred with respect to women and persons with disabilities. Women generally were paid less than men for similar work. According to the Asian Development Bank, approximately 30 percent of the economically active female population engaged in the formal economy, and a large number of these women worked in semisubsistence farming or were self-employed. Women have full rights of inheritance and property ownership by law of indigenous communal land, which constituted more than 80 percent of all land, but authorities seldom recognized this right (see section 6). The NGO Fiji Disabled People's Association reported that most persons with disabilities were unemployed due to lack of access, sufficient education and training, and discrimination by employers.

e. Acceptable Conditions of Work

In 2015 under the Employment Relations (National Minimum Wage) Regulations, the government raised the national minimum wage of F$2 ($0.97) per hour to F$2.32 ($1.13) per hour. The regulations stipulate that all employers must display a written national minimum wage notice in their workplace to inform employees of their rights. There was no up-to-date official poverty-level income figure, but the minimum wage did not typically provide a decent standard of living for a worker and family. On May 7, the FTUC launched a national campaign to increase the national minimum wage to F$4 ($1.95) per hour.

There is no single national limitation on maximum working hours for adults, but there are restrictions and overtime provisions in certain sectors. The government establishes workplace safety laws and regulations.

The Employment Ministry's Office of Labor Inspectorate is responsible for enforcing the minimum wage, but the inspectorate did not have sufficient capacity to enforce the law fully. Convictions for a breach of the minimum wage law result in a fine of F$20,000 ($9,750), two years in prison, or both. The Occupational Health and Safety Inspectorate in the Ministry of Employment monitored workplaces and equipment and investigated complaints from workers.

Government enforcement of safety standards suffered from a lack of trained personnel and delays in compensation hearings and rulings. Although mines are excluded from general workplace health and safety laws, the mining act empowers the director of mines and his inspectors to enter and inspect all mines to provide for the health, safety, and welfare of employees. The Employment Relations Tribunal and the Employment Court adjudicate cases of employers charged by the inspectorate with violating minimum wage orders and decide on workmen's compensation claims filed by the inspectorate on behalf of workers.

Unions generally monitored safety standards in organized workplaces, but many work areas did not meet standards, and the ministry did not monitor all for compliance. Workers in some industries, notably security, transportation, and shipping, worked excessive hours. According to a May 29 article in the *Fiji Sun*, four Fijian workers died in work-related incidents during the year.